W9-BMX-895

# *The* PAPERMAKERS

*Paper made by William Rittenhouse*

*COLONIAL CRAFTSMEN*

# The
# PAPERMAKERS

WRITTEN & ILLUSTRATED BY

*Leonard Everett Fisher*

**B**ENCHMARK **B**OOKS

MARSHALL CAVENDISH
NEW YORK

*For my wife, Margery*

Benchmark Books
Marshall Cavendish Corporation
99 White Plains Road
Tarrytown, NY 10591-9001

Copyright © 1965 by Leonard Everett Fisher

First Marshall Cavendish edition 2001

Library of Congress Cataloging-in-Publication Data
Fisher, Leonard Everett.
The papermakers / written and illustrated by Leonard Everett Fisher.
p. cm. — (Colonial craftsmen)
Originally published: New York : Franklin Watts, 1965.
Includes index.
ISBN 0-7614-1147-X
1. Papermaking—United States—Juvenile literature.
[1. Papermaking. 2. United States.—History.—Colonial period, ca. 1600–1755.]
I. Title.
TS1105.5 .F57    2001    676'.0973'09032—dc21    00-045158

Printed and bound in the United States of America

1    3    5    6    4    2

## Other titles in this series

# A Short History

*William Rittenhouse
arrived in 1688*

I N 1688 THERE ARRIVED IN GERMAN-Town, near Philadelphia in the Pennsylvania colony, a forty-four-year-old master craftsman. He was William Rittenhouse, a papermaker from Mulheim, in Prussia.

Not many papermakers came to America in its beginning years. The making of paper took such careful skill that few men were trained in the ancient craft. Those who were so trained found more than enough work in the European papermaking centers, and most of them saw no reason to cross the seas to an uncivilized wilderness.

Nevertheless, William Rittenhouse came to America, and one man in particular was glad that he did. That man was William Bradford, a young printer who lived in Philadelphia.

William Bradford had come to Pennsylvania in its early days. Soon he was hard at work producing pamphlets, as Philadelphia's first printer. But he found it hard to get the paper he needed for printing. Paper was scarce in the New World. Every scrap of it in the British colonies had to be imported from England.

*Rittenhouse and Bradford formed a business partnership*

*In 1690 a paper mill
was built on the banks
of Wissahickon Creek*

So, when William Rittenhouse, the papermaker, arrived in German-Town, it was not long before William Bradford, the printer, heard of him. The two men met and with some other colonists formed a business partnership for making paper.

In 1690, Rittenhouse and Bradford built a log cabin with a waterwheel on the banks of Wissahickon Creek, near German-Town. This was the first paper mill in what is now the United States of America.

The mill almost closed in 1693 when Bradford was forced to move to New York because he printed pamphlets displeasing to some of the Quakers, who had founded the Pennsylvania colony. Nevertheless, Bradford went on printing in New York, and Rittenhouse went on making his paper for some years.

As more people came to the eastern shores of North America, they found many uses for paper. Businesses grew, and the owners needed paper for writing out their sales. The colonial governments needed paper for keeping records. Printers needed paper for printing official proclamations, advertisements, pamphlets, books, and newspapers.

Surveyors needed paper for drawing maps. People everywhere needed paper for writing letters to the families and friends they had left behind in the Old World.

Almost everyone felt the lack of enough paper. And England seemed slow in sending more shipments to fill the new and much larger demand. Many people even doubted that England could really supply as much paper as was needed. In any event, early in the 1700's, other mills were built in the American colonies.

William De Wees built the second mill on Wissahickon Creek in German-Town in 1710. A third mill was built by Thomas Willcox in 1729 in Chester County, Pennsylvania. A fourth mill was also founded in Pennsylvania. It was built by a group of religious Germans called Pietists near Ephrata, in Lancaster County, in 1736.

England did not approve of these paper mills. They were making and selling a product that England herself was exporting to the colonists, and so they were competing with English business. Yet England did nothing to stop the mills from operating. She was not worried. There was

a shortage of the raw materials necessary for making paper. At that time, rags were used, and they were hard to come by for papermaking. Even though the colonists wanted paper badly, most of them did not wish to part with their old cotton and linen rags. There were too many other uses for them in the home. England went on selling her paper to the colonies without too much trouble, but not in large amounts.

The demand for paper kept growing greater. The Americans were angry with the British because the imported paper cost so much, and they were angry with themselves because they were unable to make enough paper in the colonies. From Virginia to Massachusetts the plea went out, "Save your rags." New American mills began to be built.

Now England was worried. As time went on, colonial politicians and businessmen, rich men and poor men, were producing more and more newspapers, pamphlets, and posters to make known their discontent with British rule. American mills were supplying the paper. England tried to control the production of American paper. She

passed laws to limit the amount the colonists could make. This angered the Americans even more.

In 1776, the American Revolution began. England stopped exporting paper to the colonies altogether. Rags again became scarce and, besides that, many papermakers joined the rebel fighters. The paper shortage caused terrible confusion in General Washington's armies because, for lack of paper, commanding officers could not issue the necessary written orders. Even the soldiers in the ranks suffered, as they needed paper in which to wrap the powder and bullets to load their muskets. The situation became so desperate that every soldier who was a paper craftsman was discharged from the army to make paper, and so to use his special skill in helping to win liberty.

The *HISTORY*

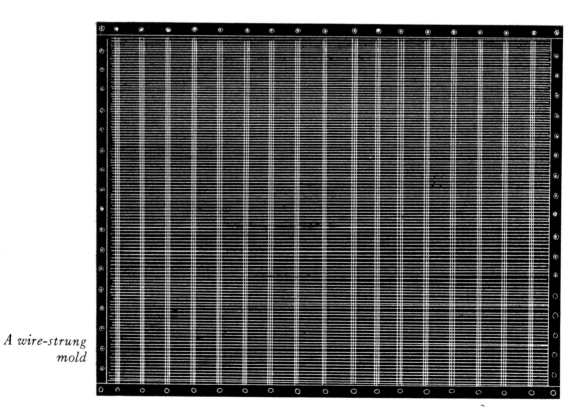

*A "T," used in hanging paper to dry*

# How the
# Papermakers Worked

PAPERMAKERS' TOOLS

*A wire-strung
mold*

**P**APER WAS INVENTED BY THE CHInese, over a thousand years before William Rittenhouse made the first piece of paper in the British American colonies.

In A.D. 105, Ts'ai Lun, a Chinese court official, mixed together the bark of mulberry trees and scraps of silk cloth and hemp and worn-out fishnets, and softened them with water. Then he pounded them until he had separated all the fibers of which they were made. Next he placed the fibers in a bucket of water, let them float to the surface, and drained the whole mixture through a screen. After he had smoothed the remaining mass of fibers out into a thin layer on the screen, he allowed it to dry in the open air. A sheet of matted material was left. This was paper.

When William Rittenhouse started his business near German-Town in 1690, he used much the same basic materials, methods, and tools as Ts'ai had so long ago.

The main papermaking fibers that the colonial American craftsmen had to use were those from cotton and linen rags. Occasionally a little jute or

*A papermaking shop*

The *TECHNIQUE*

hemp was added. The rags were collected along with other materials, and brought to the mill. There young workmen or apprentices, called *rag-pickers*, separated the cotton and linen rags from all the other stuff that had been gathered. The rags were then rolled into balls and piled in a heap.

Buckets of water were thrown onto the heap until it was well soaked. This soaking caused the rags to ferment — to go through a chemical change — and they started separating into the fibers of which they had been woven. Fermentation usually took from six to eight weeks.

When the rags had rotted sufficiently — for that is what happened to them — they were placed in hollowed-out wood or stone blocks called *vat holes*, which were part of a *stamping mill*. Here they were beaten to a pulp by large wooden hammers, until the cotton or linen fibers, once woven together, were fully separated. The stamping mill itself was operated either by hand-cranking or by a waterwheel.

Sometimes a workman shredded the rotted rags with a sharp knife before placing them in the

Waterwheel

Trip gear

Hammer

Vat hole

vat holes. In larger paper mills the wooden hammers of the stamping mill were fitted with sharp iron blades. After the blades had torn the rags apart, they were removed from the hammers, which then beat the rotted and shredded rags to pulp.

Once the rags were thoroughly pounded and their fibers were completely separated, the material was washed and stored in chests. It was called the *stock*.

When the craftsmen were ready to begin their day's work, an apprentice dipped a hand bucket into the storage chest and lifted it out, filled with stock. He dumped the stock into a large wooden tub, or *vat*, containing water. The apprentice dipped and dumped, again and again, until the proper mixture of water and stock came to within an inch or two of the top of the vat. Another workman stirred the contents of the vat from time to time, to keep the stock from settling to the bottom.

Standing in readiness on a platform directly before the vat, and waist high to its rim, was the *vatman*. He made the paper.

The vatman held in his hand a wooden frame, strung with wire and resembling a screen. This was called the *mold*. Perfectly fitted to it was a removable frame, or *deckle*, which formed a fence around the mold. It, too, was made of wood.

As soon as the mixture in the vat suited the vatman, he gripped the mold firmly, with a hand on either side. Holding it almost straight up and down, he dipped it the length of his arms into the vat. While the mold was underwater, he turned it with its deckle face up and pulled it toward him, scooping up a thin layer of wet fibers. As he lifted the mold out in a horizontal position, the deckle kept the fibers from spilling over the sides.

Now, with the mold still in a face-up position, the vatman gave it four quick, smooth shakes, from side to side and forward and backward. These shakes, called *strokes*, made the wet fibers crisscross each other, forming a strong and even sheet. The thickness of the sheet depended on the consistency of the stock and how much of it had been scooped up in the mold. The very moment that the dripping fibers were stroked and crisscrossed, they became paper.

*The coucher took the mold
from the asp
( hidden behind him in this picture )
and laid the paper on the felt*

**The TECHNIQUE**

As soon as he had finished his stroking, the vat-man removed the deckle and slid the mold with its soggy paper along a platform or bridge that ran across the top of the vat.

A second workman, called a *coucher*, picked up the mold and leaned it at an angle against an *asp*, or horn. There, more water drained from the fibers. When he judged that the mixture was dry enough, the coucher took the mold and quickly flipped it completely over, laying the wet paper flat on a woolen cloth, or *felt*, without the slightest wrinkle.

Turning the paper onto the felt was known as *couching*. As the paper was being couched, the vatman was again busy at the vat, dipping another mold for the coucher. In the meantime, the coucher had returned the first mold, which he no longer needed, to a position near the vat. There the vatman could easily pick it up and continue to make paper without interruption.

Working together, the vatman and the coucher continued to dip, stroke, drain, and couch paper until they had a pile of 144 sheets, each separated by a felt. These 144 sheets made up one *post*, or

*All the workmen*
*helped to push the press*
*down tightly*

six *quires*, according to colonial measurements. It took twenty quires, or 480 sheets, to make up one *ream* or bundle of paper. An expert team of one vatman and one coucher could produce from two to four reams of paper in a single day. The vatman's work was difficult and trying. The constant strain of plunging his arms underwater and then following the exacting motions of papermaking sometimes caused him to "lose his stroke" through paralysis.

Once a post was formed, it was very important that as much water as possible be squeezed from the paper and the felts. Otherwise, the paper would be of poor quality. To get rid of the water, the post was put in a hand-screw press, turned by a long lever. When the time came for turning the screw, all the workmen in the mill were called to help man the lever and put all their strength into pushing the press down as tightly as possible. As they worked, water ran from the paper and the felts.

When the post had been squeezed as dry as possible, another craftsman called a *layboy* or a *layman* removed it from the press. Then he sepa-

rated each piece of paper from its felt. He took great care not to tear or wrinkle the paper, and he stacked it in a neat pile with its corners and edges exactly matching.

**The** *TECHNIQUE*

After they had been separated, all the felts, which were slightly larger than the paper, were returned to the coucher.

Now the sheets of paper were again pressed, but lightly this time, and more water was removed. Next the sheets were arranged in a different order and pressed again. This reshuffling and pressing went on several more times until the paper was quite smooth. It was still damp, but the weight of the press kept it flat.

When the pressing was finished, the paper was picked up in *spurs* of four or five sheets each, and was taken to an airy room. There it was hung to dry on smooth, round rods.

As the paper dried, the marks of the wire molds became easy to see as lighter streaks, if the paper was held up to a window. Since some molds were strung differently from others, different patterns were made in the paper. A number of paper-makers bent wire into various designs and laced

*To make a watermark,
wire was bent into a design
and laced into the mold*

them into the wire-strung molds. These designs appeared in the finished paper in the same manner as the mold markings. They were called *watermarks.*

**The** *TECHNIQUE*

Designs such as birds, crowns, flowers, circles, arrows, twigs, initials, and names had been used for centuries. No one was sure of the exact meaning of some of the watermarks. Those that appeared in American colonial paper sometimes identified the papermaker, or the mill in which the paper was made. At times, a mill or a maker used a variety of watermarks, each to indicate a different quality of paper. Once in a great while, watermarks identified the person who used the paper. Both Benjamin Franklin and George Washington used writing paper especially made for them. It showed their own individual watermarks.

The completely dried paper was usually one of three colors, or shades of these colors. If the linen and cotton fibers of the rags were a light tone and the water used in the process was clear, the paper was cream-colored. If the water used was muddy, as was often the case, the paper took on a coffee

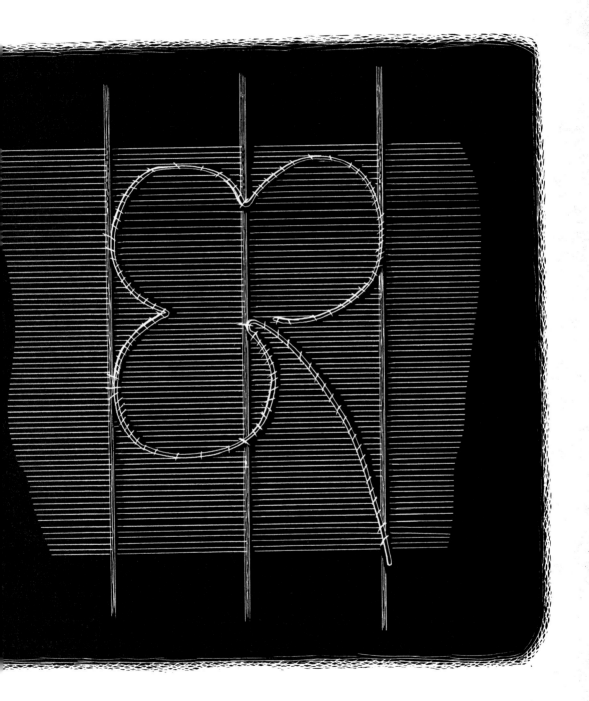

Sometimes the paper surface
was burnished with
a fine-grained stone

color. If the rag fibers were darkish and deeply discolored, either from their original dyes or from the fermentation, the paper was gray.

**The *TECHNIQUE***

When the paper was dry, it was so porous and rough that it soaked up ink almost like blotting paper, and so made writing or printing difficult, and hard to read. The paper's surface had to be hardened and made smooth in some way, in order to keep ink from spreading too much.

Sometimes the papermaker merely *burnished*, or polished, the surface of the paper with an agate or other similar fine-grained stone, to harden it. But the stone used for burnishing often made uneven shiny streaks on the paper and spoiled its appearance.

A better way to make the paper less porous and more suitable for writing or printing was to *size* it, or fill up its pores. To do this, the paper craftsman first made a warm mixture of gelatine and water called *glue size*. The gelatine was made by boiling the hides, hooves, and bones of animals. Chips of gelatine were placed in a tub of cold water, which was then heated.

As the water became hot, the gelatine dis-

*Often the paper
was dipped into sizing,
which made it less porous*

solved, forming a clear, slightly yellow liquid. As the glue-size mixture cooled, it became a little bit sticky. If it was allowed to cool entirely, it turned into a cloudy, tough, jelly-like mass. Therefore, in order to be of any use as a liquid, the glue size had to be kept warm.

The papermaker dipped the paper into the warm glue size and once again allowed it to dry. When the newly sized paper was dry, it was placed in a press, which put great force upon it. This force, or pressure, gave the paper a more even finish than rubbing with a stone did. The final finishing of paper, whether by rubbing or pressing, was called *glazing*.

In late colonial years the sized paper was run between two heavy rollers. Their steady pressure resulted in an even smoother finish than the other methods had.

Once the glazing was finished, the paper was ready to be used. Some papermakers were so careful that they insisted on trimming, or cutting off, the rough edges of the newly made sheets. These rough edges were caused by the deckle frame that the vatman had used in the very first step of

**The TECHNIQUE**

making the paper. They were therefore called *deckle edges*. It made little difference in the quality of the paper whether or not the deckle edges were cut and the paper was trimmed evenly. More often than not, the deckle edges were left untouched.

We still have many important early American letters, books, newspapers, and documents printed or written on the paper made by the colonial craftsmen. Some of the paper is discolored, and some of it is less finely finished than more modern papers are. But still, it is strong and carefully made — the product of skillful men who did excellent work with equipment that seems poor to us today. So well did the colonial American craftsmen make their paper that the valuable historical writings recorded on it will be with us for many, many years to come — a priceless heritage for us all.

# Papermaking Terms

ASP — The horn against which the mold was leaned, in order to drain water from the wet paper.

BURNISHING — Polishing the surface of paper, to harden it.

COUCHER — The workman who turned the wet paper from the mold onto the felt.

COUCHING — The process of turning the wet paper onto the felt.

DECKLE — The wooden removable frame which formed a fence around the vatman's mold.

DECKLE EDGES — The rough edges of a sheet of paper, caused by the deckle on the mold.

FELTS — The woolen cloths onto which the sheets of wet paper were turned.

GLAZING — The final finishing of the surface of a sheet of paper.

LAYMAN — The worker who removed the sheets of paper from the felts.

MOLD — The wooden frame strung with wire, which the vatman used in making paper.

POST — A pile of 144 sheets of paper, each separated by a felt.

QUIRE — Twenty-four sheets of paper.

RAGPICKERS — Apprentices who separated the cotton and linen rags from all the other material that had been collected by the papermakers.

REAM — A bundle of 480 sheets of paper: twenty quires in all.

SIZE — A warm mixture of gelatine, used to fill up the pores of the paper and make it nonabsorbent.

SPUR — A bunch of four or five sheets of paper, kept together for drying.

STAMPING MILL — The machine that beat rags to a pulp, so that they might be used in papermaking.

STOCK — The pulped and separated fiber from which paper was made.

STROKES — The shakes which the vatman gave the mold after he had scooped up the wet fibers, in order to make them crisscross each other.

VAT — The large wooden container that held the material with which the vatman worked to make paper.

VAT HOLES — Hollowed-out wood or stone blocks in which the rags were beaten to a pulp for papermaking.

VATMAN — The worker who made the paper from the mixture of stock and water in the vat.

WATERMARKS — The lighter marks made on paper by various wires strung on the mold, often in special designs.

# Some Colonial Paper Watermarks

EPHRATA MILL (1736)*
*Pennsylvania*
*(Samuel and Jacob Funk,*
*papermakers)*

BENJAMIN FRANKLIN
*(For printing paper used in*
*Franklin printing shop,*
*Philadelphia, Pennsylvania*

HEMPSTEAD HARBOR MILL (1773)
*Roslyn, Long Island, N.Y.*
*(Hendrick Onderdonk, papermaker)*

WILLIAM HOFFMAN MILL (1776)
*Maryland*
*(William Hoffman, papermaker)*

YANTIC RIVER MILL (1766)
*Norwich, Connecticut*
*(Christopher Leffingwell,*
*papermaker)*

**WILLIAM PARKS MILL (1744)**
*Williamsburg, Virginia
(Papermakers were local
citizens, probably trained by
Johann Conrad Scheetz of
Pennsylvania)*

**RITTENHOUSE MILL (1690)**
*German-Town, Pennsylvania
(Klaus Rittenhouse, papermaker)*

**RITTENHOUSE MILL (1690)**
*German-town, Pennsylvania
(William Rittenhouse, papermaker)*

**GEORGE WASHINGTON**
*(made by Hendrick Onderdonk
of Long Island for personal
letter paper, 1790)*

**WOONASQUATUCKET RIVER MILL
(1764)**
*Olneyville, Rhode Island
(John Waterman, manager)*

**IVY MILLS (1729)**
*German-Town, Pennsylvania
(Thomas Willcox, papermaker)*

# Index

LEONARD EVERETT FISHER is a well-known author-artist whose books include *Alphabet Art, The Great Wall of China, The Tower of London, Marie Curie, Jason and the Golden Fleece, The Olympians, The ABC Exhibit, Sailboat Lost,* and many others.

Often honored for his contribution to children's literature, Mr. Fisher was the recipient of the 1989 Nonfiction Award presented by the *Washington Post* and the Children's Book Guild of Washington for the body of an author's work. In 1991, he received both the Catholic Library Association's Regina Medal and the University of Minnesota's Kerlan Award for the entire body of his work. Leonard Everett Fisher lives in Westport, Connecticut.